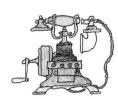

CLOTHES

THROUGH THE AGES

SIMON & SCHUSTER

First published in Great Britain in 1993 by
Simon & Schuster Young Books
Campus 400
Maylands Avenue
Hemel Hempstead
Herts HP2 7EZ

© 1992 Arnoldo Mondadori Editore S.p.A., Milan
English text © 1993 Simon & Schuster Young Books

ISBN 0 7500 1354 0

A catalogue record for this book is available from the British Library

Printed in Italy by Arnoldo Mondadori - Verona

CONTENTS

INTRODUCTION

Why do we wear clothes? Are they simply a protection from the hot sun or bitter cold, or do we use them to display ourselves, and to make others admire us? Like it or not, the clothes we wear serve all these different purposes, and have done so from the earliest times.

Many thousands of years ago people sewed animal skins together to make rough, protective clothing. Later, as they began to keep animals and grow crops, people learnt to make simple materials by spinning and weaving the threads from animal fleeces and from plants like flax and cotton. Some threads made cloth that was finer and more precious than others. Silk, for example – the glossy thread made by silkworms – has always produced beautiful but expensive cloth which only the wealthiest people could afford. In this way, clothes soon became status symbols – a way of showing the world how important and rich you were. Particular garments became status symbols, too. In Imperial Rome, for example, the toga could only be worn by Roman citizens – the upper classes in Roman society. It was like being a member of the most exclusive club.

This book tells the story of clothes. It describes how different societies have chosen to dress themselves at different times in their history, and how changing fashions and lifestyles affect the clothes that people wear.

THE FIRST CLOTHES

About 50,000 years ago Europe was a cold, hostile place to live. Although the Ice Age was coming to an end, enormous stretches of ice still covered northern lands, and dangerous animals prowled in the dark, dense forests.

Clothes of skin and fur

The earliest people where nomads who moved from place to place, following the animals they hunted – mammoths, bears, bison and reindeer. The first clothes were simply the skins of these animals, thrown over the shoulder and tied roughly round the waist. In time, however, as people learnt to make tools from bone and horn, they began to make needles. These they threaded with dried animal tendons – the string-like part of an animal's body that joins the muscles to the bones. They could then sew skins into warmer, more practical clothes.

The first jewellery

Some of the places where nomads settled many thousands of years ago have been discovered by archaeologists. As they sift through the ancient remains, they sometimes find decorated beads made from animal teeth or bone. The beads are a sign that people liked to wear beautiful things from the earliest times

People soon discovered that holding skins in the smoke of a fire helped to preserve them. The skins were then cleaned and cut with tools made of bone and flint.

ANCIENT EGYPT

This simple headdress is typical of Ancient Egypt. It is called a *nemeth*.

Clothes to keep cool

The clothes worn in Ancient Egypt were designed to suit the country's hot climate. From the very start of their civilisation, in about 3000 BC, most Egyptians wore a simple loincloth, whether they were a high-ranking official or an ordinary worker. There was a difference, however, in the quality of the material: the finest linen in the case of the ruling pharaoh and the upper classes; coarse material or leather for the ordinary people.

Linen is a fabric made from a plant called flax, which was grown in Egypt from the earliest times. It was soaked and beaten to separate its fibres, and then spun and woven to make linen.

Women's clothes

Egyptian society respected and honoured women. Perhaps this explains why their style of clothing was more refined. They too wore a simple loincloth but it was half-hidden beneath a long transparent garment called a *kalasiris*.

A *kalisiris* was made of a very fine material, dyed in a soft colour. The garment came up to below the breast, and was held either by a coloured belt or delicate shoulder straps. In a country as hot as Egypt, the *kalisiris* must have been delightfully cool to wear.

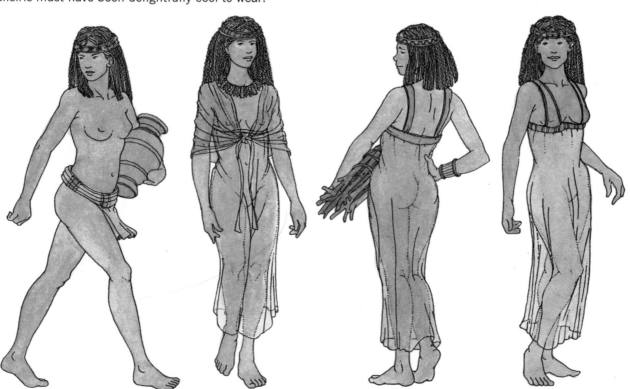

Personal adornment

Since most Egyptians walked round semi-naked, their personal appearance was extremely important to them. They liked to have smooth, hairless bodies that were scrupulously clean, and many surviving objects – like combs, mirrors, and tongs – show how hard they must have worked at this. Both men and women wore some make-up – green paint on their eyelids, and a black line round their eyes – in a style of make-up that hardly changed over thousands of years. They arranged their hair in braids or curls, or wore highly decorative wigs. They loved fine jewellery which was made of gold, semi-precious stones, or small pieces of glazed earthenware.

All loincloths had the same basic shape. They were wrapped round the waist and secured by a knot – often quite elaborately tied. The loincloth of an official (**1**) was more like a kilt, and was often beautifully pleated.

To avoid insect bites (**2**) people rubbed perfumed oil into their skin.

People wore simple sandals made of reeds (**3**), or they went barefoot.

The most ancient garment was a sheepskin skirt.

The *kandys* was a kind of tunic. Rich people wore it long, decorated with fringes. Soldiers wore it short.

This headdress was known as a *polos*.

ANCIENT MESOPOTAMIA

At about the same time as Egypt was flourishing, a wealthy civilisation was developing in Mesopotamia, a region now in southern Iraq in the Middle East. Mesopotamia lay on a large plain between two mighty rivers – the Tigris and the Euphrates. Like the River Nile in Egypt, the flooding of the rivers made the land very fertile, and Mesopotamia soon became a wealthy agricultural centre.

Many different peoples

Different groups of people held power in Mesopotamia during its long civilisation: the Sumerians, the Babylonians and the Assyrians. The region also had links with other civilisations further afield – the Hittites, the Persians and the Phoenicians, a seafaring people who traded beyond the Mediterranean Sea. In spite of this mix of peoples, Mesopotamia had its own particular style of clothing.

The clothes of Mesopotamia

The early farmers wore simple sheepskins, tied round the waist like a skirt. Later, the people of Mesopotamia began to roll the wool from their sheep into a loose yarn, and wove it into cloth. With the cloth, they made long robes, which they wore over the left shoulder and arm. The robes were often worn with a *kaunace*, a rich fringed drape made of precious wool, which was wrapped round the body in a spiral and made the wearer look stately and important. The *kaunace* was also draped over a tunic-like garment called a *kandys*, which was worn very widely throughout Mesopotamia. The *kandys* was very flexible: it was made from linen, silk or cotton; worn either long or short, with or without sleeves; it was brightly coloured, embroidered or beautifully decorated with woollen fringes – all depending on the importance of the wearer.

Phoenician women wore tight colourful skirts. They arranged their hair in braids or in a turban.

The Persians wore soft cloth trousers, known as *anaxyrides*, with a short *kandys* and a long cloak.

The Phoenicians were famous for their dyed cloth. The most highly prized colour was purple.

Assyrian men grew their hair and beards long, perfumed them with oil, and bound them with gold thread. A metal headband stopped the hair falling over the face.

TANNING LEATHER

After the animal had been killed, it was skinned carefully to avoid damaging the hide.

Its hide was scraped clean against a tree trunk to get rid of any flesh, fat or hairs.

Holes were punched along the outside edge of the skins. They could then be sewn together.

Although leather was used widely by the Romans, it was only during the conquest of Britain in AD 43 that they first saw it being used for clothes.

Leather can sometimes be as soft as a fabric. It can then be sewn with finer needles and made into elegant lightweight clothing for women.

It seems that as soon as people learned to hunt, they began to use animal skins to make leather. This is clear from the discovery of Stone Age bone and flint scrapers. What is less clear is when people first learnt the art of tanning.

The history of tanning

The skin of any animal contains water and will rot quickly if it is just left. To make it last, it has to go through a process called tanning. Tanning can be done in various different ways. One of the first ways to be tried thousands of years ago

was to hold an animal hide very tautly and rub fat into it. Later, oil was used for this kind of tanning.

Another way to tan leather is to use a natural substance found in the ground, called alum. This was the method used by the Ancient Egyptians. Hides tanned with alum tend to harden, which made the leather particularly suitable for shoes. Alum also turns the leather white, a good base colour for the Egyptian dyers who dyed leather yellow, green or blue.

A third way to tan leather is to use tannic

Leather was also preserved by soaking and airing.
Spreading salt on the leather dried it out completely.

acid, now known as tannin. This substance is made from bark (particularly oak tree bark), roots, leaves and fruits. Historians know that tannin was used in Mesopotamia, and that large oak woods were planted for this purpose.

These three different tanning methods were still being used in the 19th century (1800–1900). Each method gave the leather a different colour: oil tanning turned it brown; alum left it white; and the vegetable tannins coloured it a whole range of shades from beige to a deep reddish-brown.

The use of leather

In the Stone Age pieces of leather were sewn together to make simple clothes. Leather was also used for containers and, in time, there were many kinds of bags for carrying such different things as water or grain.

In Egypt leather was used for sandals, clothes and cushions. It may even have been used to make gloves.

In Mesopotamia the Babylonians became skilled craftsmen in leather. Their red goatskin shoes, decorated with jewels and embroidery, were so famous that even the Roman Emperors wore them!

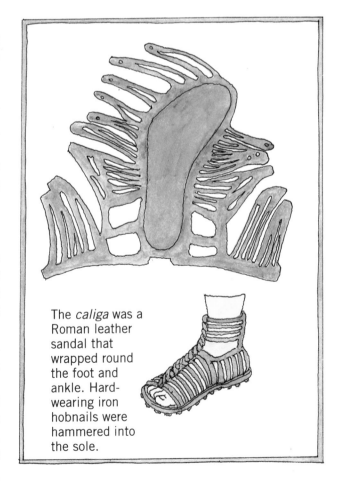

The *caliga* was a Roman leather sandal that wrapped round the foot and ankle. Hard-wearing iron hobnails were hammered into the sole.

Like the Egyptians, the Cretans took great care with their personal appearance.

Wealthy people wore hats of many different designs – often held in place with a gold hat pin.

Elegant women wore long, flounced skirts made of beautiful materials. Their long hair hung loose or was tied back with ribbons, hairpins or in a hairnet.

ON THE ISLAND OF CRETE

The island of Crete lies in the Mediterranean Sea. It has a good climate and rich soil, and in about 2000 BC it had a glittering civilisation. Thanks to the island's position, the Cretans travelled widely, trading with Greece, Egypt and Syria. They became wealthy, and developed a rich culture. Paintings on the walls of the island's palaces show some of the island's liveliest occasions, including bull-leaping – a terrifying sport in which young men and women somersaulted over the horns of a charging bull.

Men's clothes
In summer the young men wore little more than a loincloth, perhaps decorated with beads, and a well-made pair of leather sandals. In winter the loincloth was replaced with a longer garment like a skirt or a pair of shorts, or wide knee-length trousers. Well-to-do men wore a wool or fur shawl and a pair of fine leather boots on their feet. Poorer men made do with a simple knee-length tunic made of linen.

Women's clothes
Women had an important role in Cretan society, and the clothes they wore were colourful, detailed and lively. Upper-class women wore long skirts with multi-coloured layers, and a tight belt to show off their slim waist. On their top half they wore boleros – tight-fitting bodices which fastened below the breast and had elbow-length sleeves. Over their skirt they wore a small apron, which was embroidered on the front and back.

Ordinary women did not wear such exotic clothes. Like the men, they wore simple linen tunics, which came down to the ankle, and tied at the waist with a belt.

Dress materials were dyed in the richest colours. Two strongly contrasting shades were used in a garment – red and orange, or blue and green – to achieve new and exciting effects.

The fashions worn on the island of Crete were remarkably imaginative. No other ancient civilisation produced such lively, colourful clothes.

When a *chiton* was made out of particularly fine material, it was sometimes draped to make false sleeves which covered the arms.

Cloth for the *chiton* and *himation* was white at first, but was later dyed. Bright colours were especially popular.

The *peplos* was a fuller tunic. It was sometimes sewn down one side, and had extra material over the top half of the body.

Heads and headdresses

◀ Greek women wore their hair long. A popular style was to pile it up at the back of the head in a hairnet. Rich women wore gold decorations in their hair on special occasions.

◀ All manner of hats were worn, in styles from as far afield as Egypt, the Middle East and the Far East.

▶ Blond hair was much admired. Both men and women dried their hair in the sun to try and lighten it.

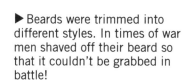

▶ Beards were trimmed into different styles. In times of war men shaved off their beard so that it couldn't be grabbed in battle!

The cloth was dyed or embroidered with spirals, rectangles, and zig-zags – patterns which are still popular in Greece today.

Expensive silks and cottons were imported from the East. They must have been light and cool to wear in the hot summer.

Men sometimes wore a short *chiton,* or a *himation* on its own. They went barefoot at home, but wore sandals when they went out.

GREEK FASHION

An elegant simplicity
The Greeks valued simplicity and grace in their dress. Look at the sculptures and vases of the time, and you will see men and women in elegant, softly-folded garments. This style of dress hardly changed, even as the Greek people grew richer. The basic garments were much the same for both men and women – a simple tunic called a *chiton* which fastened at the shoulders, and a cloak flung over the top.

Women's style
Women wore the *chiton* long. It was made of two rectangles of cloth, fastened gracefully along the arms and shoulders, and tied at the waist. It was usually made out of finely spun wool, but as people grew richer and could afford better quality material which hung better, it became more elaborate with various pleats and gathers.

A square woollen wrap was often worn over the top.

Women wore simple underwear under their clothes. This wasn't fitted, like underwear today. A bra, for example, was just a strip of material wound tightly around the body. Other strips of material were tied round the body like bandages to make the woman look thinner.

Men's style
Men wore the *chiton* shorter than women. Over the top, they might wear a *himation,* a wide rectangular piece of material which served as a cloak. In warm weather men might wear nothing but the *himation,* wound loosely round their body and over the left shoulder. Young men and soldiers often wore a shorter cloak called a *chlamys,* which was fastened at the shoulder with a buckle.

THE CLOTHES OF ROME

Hats were rare in Rome. A traveller might wear a wide-brimmed hat with a cloak, some simple leggings and a pair of solid shoes.

A woman's working garment was a simple sleeveless tunic gathered at the waist.

The toga was more than a piece of clothing – it was a symbol of freedom. As such, it could only be worn by a Roman citizen.

It was made of a length of white wool, draped over the left arm and shoulder.

Spinning, weaving and making clothes were traditional tasks for even the wealthiest women.

Simple cloth, simple styles

Most Roman clothing was made of homespun wool or linen. Like Greek clothing, the garments were simple – just pieces of cloth draped loosely round the body. The cloth itself was fairly narrow at first because it was woven at home on small looms. In time, however, when the design of looms changed, it could be woven in wider pieces which then hung in deeper, richer folds.

Both men and women wore simple tunics with different types of cloaks. Young women wore a long sleeveless tunic which looked rather like a petticoat. Older women wore a fuller tunic on the top, called a *stola*. Men's clothes were very similar. They wore a knee-length tunic, though on special occasions Roman citizens wore a long white toga. Trousers were considered uncivilised, and were worn only by travellers or people who worked outdoors.

ROMAN SOCIETY

The social classes

Roman society lived according to certain rules. There was a clear and definite social scale, and every person knew where he or she stood. At the top of the scale were the patricians. They were the wealthiest, most privileged families whose men became senators and governed the Empire. Below the patricians were the Roman citizens – wealthy aristocrats and powerful members of the armed forces. Next came the ordinary, free people of Rome – the soldiers and merchants – and the freed slaves. At the bottom of the scale were the slaves, who did most of the hard work in the Empire and who were sometimes rewarded with their freedom.

Clothes in society: the toga

Clothes soon became a sure way of recognising the social class of the person who was wearing them. The toga, for example, could only be worn by wealthy Roman citizens – never by foreigners, slaves or freed men. The colour of a toga was another way of distinuishing people. The Roman Emperor wore purple, while senators, magistrates, priests and the young sons of Roman citizens wore white togas with a purple band – the width of the band depending on the person's importance in society. The togas of public officials were plain white; if an official wore brown it was because he was mourning the death of a relative.

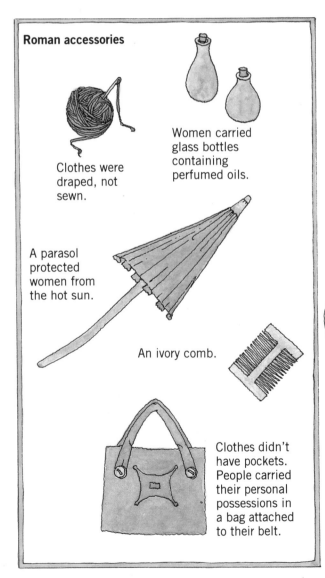

Roman accessories

Clothes were draped, not sewn.

Women carried glass bottles containing perfumed oils.

A parasol protected women from the hot sun.

An ivory comb.

Clothes didn't have pockets. People carried their personal possessions in a bag attached to their belt.

Chariot racing was popular. A charioteer wore a leather hat and strips of leather to protect his body. A spray of laurel was given to the winner.

Clothing across the classes

Patricians and generals

Free people and freed slaves

| Standard-bearer | Peasant | Gladiator | Actor | Dancer | Innkeeper |

The cut of a cloak

The toga wasn't the only garment which varied according to people's social class. Different kinds of cloak also showed people's rank or profession. Scholars and senators, for example, wore a cloak which hung from the left shoulder, while a soldier's cloak hung from the right. Patricians had cloaks with hoods to protect them from the rain; servants' cloaks were nothing more than a square of cloth with a hole for the head. Wealthy women wore a large brightly-coloured cloak called a *pella* over their tunic, which they used to cover their head when they went out. The *pella* was made of colourful cloth and perhaps embroidered or decorated with tassels. A general alone could wear a purple cloak, while the cloak belonging to the Emperor was twice as large and very richly decorated.

Even the shoes you wore on your feet showed people which social class you belonged to: senators wore black shoes; patricians' shoes were red; and wealthy women wore red and gold shoes, studded with precious stones.

Hairstyles

Men wore their hair short, and either clipped their beards or were clean-shaven. Wealthy women dyed their hair and wore it in formal, complicated styles. They pinned it up at the back – building it up with extra hairpieces if necessary – keeping a mass of curls around the face. Beautiful hair ornaments of gold and bronze were widely worn. As with clothes, there were certain social rules about which rank of woman could wear which kind of hairstyle; the more complicated styles were reserved for the rich and powerful. Different fashions in hairstyles changed quite rigidly with the passing years. They are now used by museum curators as a way of dating statues, vases and paintings.

Long cloaks were held at the shoulder by beautiful pins and brooches.

A *tablion* was a decorative panel sewn into a cloak. It was often magnificently embroidered.

A tunic was sometimes tucked into the colourful leggings.

Clothes were often decorated with geometric designs – squares, diamonds and circles.

This colourful outfit, decorated with gold braid, would have been worn by an important official.

Long loose robes were worn by priests. They were eventually worn by ordinary people, too.

Many women covered their head and shoulders with a loose veil.

The Empress wore a long trailing cloak. Her crown was made of precious stones and metals.

Women wore their hair up – in ribbons or a hairnet that glittered with gems.

ANCIENT BYZANTIUM

A richer style

In AD 330 the Roman Emperor Constantine moved his capital city from Rome to Byzantium (in the country which is now Turkey). Local tastes gradually began to change the Roman style of dress. Clothes which had draped softly round the body now had a sharper look, giving them a grander, more powerful appearance. Although many garments were still made from wool and linen, wealthy people began to wear damask, a rich highly patterned cloth. Silk was so expensive that it was only worn by the wealthiest people in the land.

Men's clothes

Men wore a short tunic gathered at the waist with a belt, over a pair of colourful leggings. The rich wore a wide silk sash over their tunic, encrusted with gold and precious stones. They also wore a long cloak with a decorative panel sewn into it, known as a *tablion.*

Shoes were made of silk or soft leather. The Emperor's shoes were purple, and richly decorated with gold buckles and jewels. The shoes worn by important officials were usually black.

Women's clothes

Wealthy women wore long loose-fitting tunics, one on top of another. The under-tunic had close-fitting sleeves; the over-tunic was fuller and very decorative. Many fabrics had a raised pattern, known as embossing, or were embroidered with plants and flowers, or with geometric patterns, like circles and squares.

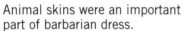
Animal skins were an important part of barbarian dress.

Men wore furs over their tunics to protect them from the cold winter weather. Leather was used for belts and cloaks. Goatskin was used for trousers.

The barbarians invaded Italy and other parts of the Roman Empire until it finally collapsed. Then they settled down and lived much as they had before, while the great Roman buildings crumbled around them.

Women wore a short shirt tucked into a skirt. Later the shirt became as long as a dress.

The barbarians were talented metalworkers. They used metal for weapons, armour, clasps and jewellery. Their bronze helmets were decorated with animal horns.

THE BARBARIANS

Invading the Empire

By the fourth century (AD 300–400) the great Roman Empire was beginning to collapse. The people that lived on its borders now began to invade and destroy its cities, attacking the inhabitants and stealing their goods. The invaders came from many different tribes, each with its own particular culture, but we now call them by a single name – 'the barbarians'.

Clothes for the North

Since the barbarian tribes lived largely in the North, they needed clothes that would keep out the cold. They wore thicker fabrics and warm furs instead of the fine linen of the South. Although their clothing looks simple, it improved on Roman methods in an important way. The barbarians cut cloth in order to make their garments, while the Romans simply folded a piece of material round themselves. Clothes made of different pieces which are sewn together are stronger, warmer and much more useful.

Men wore a short woollen tunic with holes for the head and the arms, and a second tunic of fur or leather. On their legs they wore long trousers and high leather boots. Women's clothing was very similar, but their tunics were ankle-length, and were often covered by a cloak.

A finer touch

As the barbarian tribes came into contact with Roman civilisation, their style of dress began to change. It became more attractive and comfortable. People started to use finer fabrics and put sleeves in their garments. They decorated them with trimmings, and began to wear jewellery made with multi-coloured stones.

THE STORY OF WOOL

It was the women of Greece and Rome who perfected the art of spinning and weaving wool. They were constantly looking for ways to make softer, finer fabrics and soon learnt which breeds of sheep produced the best fleeces. Some women even made coats for sheep out of animal skins in order to protect the fleece that was growing underneath.

Preparing the fleece
The sheep were shorn in the springtime. The fleeces were carefully examined and their wool was graded according to its quality. The wool was then washed several times to remove any fat, sweat or bits of grass. To untangle it, the wool had to be combed with a special comb. This process is called carding, and it produces long straight threads ready for spinning.

Spinning the yarn
Civilisations all over the world have used the same tools for spinning – a spindle and a distaff. The tools hardly changed from Greek times, in about 500 BC, until the 15th century (AD 1400–1500) about 2000 years later. The carded wool was wound round the distaff and a loose strand was attached to the spindle, which was then set spinning. As it spun, the spindle wound the wool into yarn ready for weaving.

Weaving the cloth
The yarn was woven on a good-sized loom to make wide pieces of cloth. The newly woven cloth was washed, soaked and beaten to fluff up the fibres and hide the weave. The last step would be to dye the cloth with vegetable or animal colouring. It could then be made into clothes.

The wool was cleaned and combed and wound round a long distaff. A single strand of wool was then twisted round the spindle to make yarn.

Tools for shearing first appeared in Roman times. Until then, the fleece was pulled out rather than cut.

There were simple tools for carding the wool fleece. They were made of wood and had a head of metal 'teeth'.

A row of threads, known as the warp, was stretched on the loom. The yarn was threaded through them – over and under, over and under – to form the crossways thread, known as the weft.

Red was a difficult colour to dye clothes because it soon turned to pink. One of the most common red dyes was obtained from an insect.

THE DARK AGES

It wasn't just buildings and cities that were attacked by the barbarians. They also destroyed the Roman way of life. Many of the invading tribes were nomads, living a very different kind of life from the law and order of Roman towns and cities.

A time of chaos

After its collapse, the Roman Empire broke up into many separate kingdoms. Cities were abandoned, crafts were forgotten, roads and bridges crumbled. Trade collapsed and people had to make their living from the land. In constant fear of attack, people begged protection from powerful lords who built well-defended castles. This period of history – from about AD 500–900 – is called the Dark Ages because the learning of Ancient Greece and Rome almost disappeared. In its place the Christian Church began to give leadership to people. Its monasteries were centres of learning, offering a quiet life behind protective stone walls.

Feudal society

King

Pope

Lords of the manor

High churchmen

Knights and vassals

Clergymen and monks

Peasants and serfs

Travelling in the Dark Ages
The few roads that existed were in a poor condition, and infested with robbers. No wonder people hardly stirred from the land that surrounded their lord's castle. They would only travel when there was a fair near by. Fairs were a rare opportunity to see goods from abroad, and sell surplus food, cloth or other homemade goods.

A hard life

Most people were too careworn to think about the clothes they wore. Their homemade garments were dingy, rough and shapeless – a protection from the weather and nothing more. Men wore a short wool or linen tunic over simple trousers. Women wore long tunics tied at the waist, with an extra wool or fur shawl in the winter. Shoes were made from pieces of leather wrapped round the foot and tied on with straps.

From serf to king

Just as Roman society had had its different classes, ranging from slaves right up to the Emperor, so society in the early Middle Ages had them, too. At the top of the scale was the king. He gave powerful noblemen large pieces of land on which they built castles and became lords of the manor. In turn, these lords gave pieces of land to lesser nobles and knights, who became the lord's vassals and promised to fight for him when necessary. Below the vassals were the peasants and serfs who scratched a living from strips of land, and paid taxes to the lord in the form of work and goods. This kind of society, where land is given in return for goods and services, is known as a feudal system. It was widespread throughout Europe at this time.

A glimpse of luxury

People who were higher up the social scale had more money than those below. This would have been obvious from the clothes they wore. However, there were few luxuries to be bought in western Europe – even by the rich. A much higher standard of living existed in Byzantium in the East, or in the Arab regions of North Africa and Spain. People here could obtain luxury items and perhaps sell them on to people in the North, but there were no regular trade routes. No wonder then that when a merchant arrived at a village or castle and showed off a piece of shiny silk or damask, an embroidered tunic or a pair of fine leather shoes, they were like a glimpse of a different world.

It wasn't until about AD 950, when the last barbarian invasion was defeated, that the Dark Ages finally came to an end. People could now live more confidently – free from fear, and ready to enjoy the more beautiful things in life.

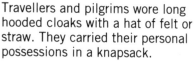

Travellers and pilgrims wore long hooded cloaks with a hat of felt or straw. They carried their personal possessions in a knapsack.

The belted tunic was a typical garment of this time. It was often worn over cloth stockings with cork soles.

Hats were sometimes worn over a short cloak that veiled the head.

THE MIDDLE AGES

Life steadily improved for most people after the Dark Ages. Cities revived, arts and crafts began to flourish, people travelled more widely, and trade routes became established.

Luxuries from the East
In 1095 the pope, who was the Head of the Christian Church, appealed to Christians to recapture the holy city of Jerusalem from the Turkish Muslims who had seized it. Thousands of people – knights, princes and peasants – set out on a long warring pilgrimage, called a crusade. It was the first of eight crusades that took place over the next 200 years. Although the crusades were not successful, they had a surprising and long-lasting effect on life in northern Europe. The returning crusaders brought home with them a taste for the civilised lifestyle of the Arabs – for their silks and spices, fine rugs, metalwork and glass.

Dressing with care
The new wealth and more bustling lifestyle of the towns and cities, encouraged people to dress with greater care. Most people wore a white linen shirt with close-fitting sleeves beneath a calf-length or full-length tunic called a *gonelle*. The *gonelle* was often decorated with beautiful embroidery, colourful braids or richly coloured cloth panels. An embroidered belt was draped loosely round the waist or hips. Below the *gonelle*, men wore leggings or knee-length breeches with socks or boots.

The well-to-do classes of society wore precious fur robes that were lined in scarlet. Fur trimmings gave a touch of luxury to hats, cuffs, collars and silk shoes. Just as luxurious were the rubies, diamonds and other precious jewels that were now being imported from the East and made into jewellery of all kinds – clasps, necklaces, buckles, earrings and rings.

Ordinary people wore rough woollen breeches. Those worn by the rich were made of linen or silk.

Clothes were now dyed in richer colours, and decorated with embroidery, borders and frills.

Musicians, minstrels and dancers wore brightly coloured make-up to add to their good cheer.

Most people wore a cloak; women used a corner of theirs to veil their head.

Breeches that were tied at the knee and high leather boots were a sign of taste and wealth.

THE LATE MIDDLE AGES

A lord's tunic and cloak became longer and more colourful, and were sometimes decorated with contrasting borders.

Women's clothes

Women's robes became so long that they began to trail behind them in a train. Women liked to hold up a corner of their robe to show the contrasting colour underneath.

Buttons were introduced at this time. Clothes could now fit the body more closely without the need for a belt.

Hats were only worn by married women, and often with a wimple – a length of cloth wound round the head. Unmarried women wore their hair loose or in braids.

Long hooded cloaks were very common.

A short tunic and cloak over close-fitting hose were more practical clothes to work in.

Women wore a simple tunic at home. When they went out, they put on an outer robe and a hooded cloak.

In the 13th and 14th centuries (1200–1400) most people's standard of living was steadily improving, and this showed in the clothes they wore. Luxurious fabrics like muslin and silk were now widely available thanks to trade with the East. In Europe new cotton weaves and velvets were being produced, with designs of squares, circles and polka dots.

Clothes for the rich

Well-to-do men wore a linen or silk shirt and tight-fitting leggings, known as hose. Over this they wore a long flared tunic and an embroidered robe of wool, linen or silk, tied at the waist with a leather belt. A long fur-lined cloak hung from their shoulders.

Women's clothes were very similar to men's. They wore the same shirt and hose, a fuller tunic and a full-length robe with detachable sleeves. Both men and women carried their personal possessions in small bags attached to their belt.

Clothes for the poor

Styles of dress changed more slowly for the poor. Men still wore a simple smock, rough leggings and breeches tucked into their boots. Women wore leggings, a tunic and a long hooded cloak.

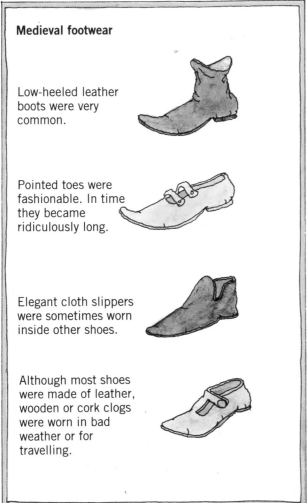

Medieval footwear

Low-heeled leather boots were very common.

Pointed toes were fashionable. In time they became ridiculously long.

Elegant cloth slippers were sometimes worn inside other shoes.

Although most shoes were made of leather, wooden or cork clogs were worn in bad weather or for travelling.

The close-fitting garments worn at this time required the skill of professional tailors, whose fees were often laid down by law. The best tailors worked in shops in the city – in an Aladdin's cave full of fine fabrics.

MERCHANTS AND TAILORS

The textile industry

During the 1400s the textile industry saw an explosion of new skills and ideas. Italy – with its good trading relations with the East – lay at the heart of the textile trade. Here and elsewhere, dress fabrics were being made to the highest standards of design and manufacture. The Italian city of Milan was famous for its velvet, and there was great demand for Italian silks and cotton weaves. The city of Venice produced wonderful velvet brocades – a deep-piled fabric with raised patterns woven in gold and silver threads. Some of the designs were drawn up by famous painters of the day.

Craftsmen of fashion

Town dwellers admired the new fabrics and were eager to wear the latest styles. Good tailors were in great demand. Working beneath the sign of a pair of scissors, they took great pride in their ability to cut fabric with style and skill. Alongside the tailors was a whole range of other craftsmen and women: dyers, knitters, furriers, cap-makers, cobblers, and so on. Haberdashers' shops were bursting with fine fabrics, ready-made clothes and accessories as well as needles, scissors and all the other tools necessary for making what had now become very complicated clothes.

Across Europe, trading centres with strong links with the East saw a huge growth in the textile trade. The largest centres were Venice, Florence and Bruges in what is now Belgium.

A New Age

New ideas

By the end of the 1400s society was changing. The huge growth in trade had created a wealthy class of townspeople who no longer fitted into the old feudal system. Indeed, many merchants now dressed and lived more luxuriously than the nobles.

People's attitude to the world was also changing. At the beginning of the Middle Ages people had believed that their place in society – whether they were a nobleman or a peasant – was decided by God. Now, however, new ideas were taking root. People began to see that they could improve their lives through their own efforts, rather than wait for their reward in heaven. The importance of such changes is hard for us to understand, but it was ideas like this that helped to shape the modern world.

New clothes

As society changed, so too did the clothes people wore. Instead of a tunic, men now wore a short, tight-fitting waistcoat called a doublet, and a pair of breeches. In Italy breeches were tight; elsewhere they were fuller with gaping slashes. Sleeves were richly decorated with trimmings and slashes which showed the white shirt underneath.

Women's clothes were more fitted than in the past, and had tight bodices – a fashion which encouraged women to wear uncomfortable corsets in the hope of looking slimmer. Necklines were cut much lower and were sometimes covered with a veil or flimsy undershirt. Sleeves were one of the most decorative features of women's dresses. They came in many styles: full, tight-fitting or gathered, and perhaps slashed and trimmed with colourful braids or fur.

The best clothes were made in rich fabrics like damask, taffeta and every kind of silk. The slashes in sleeves, doublets and breeches allowed the soft silks to puff out from underneath.

Clothes were becoming much more decorative. Accessories like jewellery, gloves, hats and bags all added to the effect.

Hairstyles and headdresses

Men wore their hair short. They had short beards or were clean-shaven.

Women arranged their long hair in a variety of styles.

During the 1500s – in the period known as the Renaissance – Italian architects began to design buildings which copied those of Ancient Greece and Rome. Their splendid, simple lines contrasted strongly with the fussy extravagance of the court.

POWER DRESSING IN THE 1500S

People of wealth and status had been using clothes to display their power since the first days of the Roman Empire. In Europe in the 1500s, however, the habit was carried to extremes.

A law of luxury

Trade was now growing at such a rate that many classes of society were becoming very wealthy and could afford more and more luxurious goods. Lucrezia Borgia, a famous Italian beauty and one of the most elegant women of the age, was said to possess over 50 gowns – many embroidered with gold and silver thread – and 90 pairs of shoes!

Members of the nobility began to resent the style and splendour of the wealthy middle classes and they passed laws which limited the amount of money people could spend on themselves. In Venice, for example, only the doge – the highest official in the land – was allowed the greatest luxuries, although noble families were entitled to wear gold and silver fabrics in his presence. However, the finery of the court was still enough to amaze King Henry III of France when he visited Venice in 1574. He said that the noblewomen's "collars, corsets and sleeves were all covered in jewels, pearls and gold."

Regal or ridiculous?

Another way to display power was to appear wider and taller than everyone else. A noblewomen must have felt like a queen in her farthingale – a stiff underskirt with whalebone hoops which greatly widened the spread of a skirt. But a frame for the bodice that was stiffened with sharpened steel was considered so dangerous that it was prohibited! With their wide sleeves and elaborate style women could not fail to look proud and important. Many people suffered in their attempts to look splendid, and they must have ended up looking ridiculous. This wish to stand out in a crowd created a style of dressing that was very different from the practical, comfortable clothes of the past.

King

Pope

High aristocracy

Merchants and bankers

Professionals, churchmen, artists, scholars, craftsmen

Peasants, labourers and servants

Clothes for the professions

Away from the excesses of the court, however, not all garments were extravagant or eccentric. Many people wore sober clothes that reflected their role in society. In fact, many garments were little more than uniforms. Styles and colours became closely linked to the work people did, just as they had done in the days of Imperial Rome. For example, in Venice the colour of a cloak was highly significant: doctors wore purple, generals wore turquoise, while most ordinary people settled for brown. The colour of a gown was equally revealing: a scholar wore red, a lawyer wore black.

Renaissance society

Renaissance society was made up of different classes of people, who enjoyed different standards of living. Thanks to the growth in trade, merchants and bankers had become wealthy and powerful members of society. This was a great change from the feudal society of the Middle Ages (see page 26), when land and wealth was handed down as a favour in return for goods and services.

16TH-CENTURY FASHION

Followers of fashion

Wealthy people's taste for elegance resulted in clothes that were becoming more and more ornate. The fabrics themselves were extremely rich. Heavy brocades were painstakingly decorated with embroidery, lace and precious jewels.

Fashion was news. Wealthy ladies started to exchange dolls that were dressed in the latest style. The first fashion magazines were now circulating widely among the well-to-do, thanks to the recent invention of the printing press.

Women's style

Women's gowns had a tight bodice and a rich, full skirt. The bodice had a very low neckline and was stiffened with whalebone. The skirt was supported by a stiff underskirt. The sleeves of the gown could be removed, revealing the white linen chemise that women wore underneath. The chemise was so popular at this time, that it was even worn in bed.

Hats were popular in England. They were made of a simple cap framed with a length of precious material.

Men's style

Men, too, wore a simple linen chemise under their doublet. Doublets were dressy garments, with sleeves that puffed out and were gathered at the wrist. On their bottom half men wore knee-length skirts or breeches with close-fitting stockings. The shoes of the period were wide with rounded toes, and were often as decorative as the clothes.

Elegant accessories

Accessories were important. Jewellery was widely worn, particularly heavy gold chains. Gloves were often carried in a bag along with the latest invention – the wildly inaccurate pocket watch. The finishing touch was some heavy perfume like civet, amber or musk (made from extracts of plants and animals). Generous amounts of it were poured onto hats, gloves, stockings and shoes; in fact the more perfume people used, the less they washed!

Women wore high ruff collars for many years but the fashion for high platform shoes soon died out.

Heads and headdresses

The strong simple lines of a headdress emphasised a woman's features.

Women brushed back their hair under linen or silk hats, with or without a veil.

Men also wore the low necklines that revealed the chemise.

Longer tunics were still worn by the upper classes with a fur-trimmed cloak, perhaps, and a hat decorated with ostrich feathers.

Spanish fashion

Dutch fashion

CLOTHES IN THE 1600S

In the early 1600s Spain was the most powerful and important country in Europe. The discovery and plunder of America had brought huge wealth into the country and given its people a taste for luxury. Spain soon became a cultural leader, and its fashions and manners were copied everywhere.

The Spanish style

Spanish fashions were rather sombre and severe. The clothes were stiff and padded, and must have been uncomfortable to wear. Everyone – even toddlers and children – wore a high ruff collar which came up to below the ear, making it almost impossible to smile or move naturally.

Men's clothes

All men wore a chemise with a high ruff. On top of this they wore a padded doublet with a high collar set under the chin. Their breeches were padded, and were worn over close-fitting stockings and ornate shoes. To finish the outfit, men wore a short cloak made of stiff silk.

Women's clothes

Women wore a tight-fitting bodice that contrasted strongly with their full skirt. In fact, women wore several skirts: on the top was an overskirt which draped over a second skirt of contrasting colour; below the second skirt were stiff petticoats; and below the petticoats was the farthingale – a cone-shaped frame that was stiffened by hoops of cane or whalebone.

The Dutch style

By the mid-1600s a new country in Europe was growing in wealth and importance – the Netherlands. It had once been part of the Spanish Empire, but had now broken away and was becoming the great trading centre of Europe. The Dutch style of dress was looser and more comfortable than the Spanish, with less stiffness and padding. Men's breeches, for example, were longer and softer, and were tucked inside soft leather boots. The high neck ruff went out of fashion and was replaced with soft collars and low necklines. Clothing was becoming lighter.

Lace was so popular in the Netherlands that it was worn everywhere – on collars, cuffs, gloves, handkerchiefs and shoes.

In northern Europe people still wore fur in the winter, and thick woollen shawls.

Peasants needed simple, practical clothes to work in.

THE SUN KING

Louis XIV (the fourteenth) was king of France from 1643 until 1715. His court at Versailles was the most magnificent in Europe, and France became the centre of civilised life. It was the splendour of both his personal appearance and his court that earned Louis XIV the name of 'the Sun King'.

French fashion

Louis XIV was clever. He quickly found that clothes were one way of controlling the powerful members of the aristocracy. He encouraged a style of dress that was flamboyant and ornate, forcing people to spend huge amounts of time and money on clothes whose styles changed constantly. Men's clothes were much fussier than women's. A short buttoned doublet was worn open over a chemise. With this, men wore skirt-like breeches called rhinegraves that were tied at the knee by a ribbon, and decorated with lace and frills. Their silk

Boots were now out of fashion. Louis XIV wore silk stockings to show off his perfectly-shaped legs.

The stiff ruff gave way to large lace collars, and to other smaller collars of different designs.

By the end of the 1600s men were wearing a silk necktie known as a cravat.

stockings and square-toed shoes were made of matching silk or velvet, and decorated with jewels. Every piece of clothing and every accessory was beautifully embroidered – the chemise, doublet, breeches, shoes and gloves.

Women's clothes

Women's clothes were simpler and more elegant than men's. They wore lower necklines than in the past – so low, in fact, that many gowns had no shoulders in them at all. Women still wore two, or even three skirts that were folded back and held in place with ribbons, clasps and pins. Their stockings were made of white or flesh-coloured silk, and their square-toed shoes were made of the same material as their dress.

Men grew their hair long, or wore a wig. They dressed in an open doublet, flounced breeches and a shoulder cloak.

In Louis XIV's reign men's clothes were covered with frills and bows. The king wore high-heeled shoes to disguise how short he was.

The French preferred light, bright colours – unlike the sombre clothes of the Spanish.

Children's clothes were becoming a little simpler, but were still basically a copy of adult styles.

The elegant clothes were worn with stylish accessories: silk parasols, feathered hats and muffs.

Women's tall headdresses were made of stiffened linen, folded into waves and bows.

THE EARLY 1700s

During the 1700s there was a slow move towards less extravagant clothes. In fact, three new garments that were introduced at this time are still worn today: the jacket, waistcoat and trousers.

Clothes for men

The short doublet was now replaced by an elegant knee-length coat of colourful brocade. It was slightly fitted at the waist and then flared to the knee, with a vent at the back for easy movement. Sleeves were narrower and plainer than in the past, but often ended in a deep cuff, trimmed with braid. Under the jacket men wore a beautiful silk shirt decorated with heavy lace cuffs, and a knee-length waistcoat that buttoned down the front. The style of breeches also changed. No longer full and padded, they were narrow knee-length trousers known as culottes. They were worn over colourful silk stockings and high-heeled shoes, decorated with buckles or rosettes.

Clothes for women

Women's clothing changed more slowly. Their gowns had the same basic shape: a close-fitting bodice and a full skirt over a stiff petticoat of contrasting colour. Sleeves were worn to the elbow and trimmed with lace.

Such formal, elaborate clothes must have been tiring and uncomfortable to wear. No wonder women welcomed a new comfortable garment known as a negligé. It was light and loose – ideal for relaxing in at home but useful for travelling, too. It was soon being worn throughout most of Europe.

The finishing touch

The 1700s was a time of elegant accessories – pretty silk umbrellas and parasols that matched women's dresses, and fans made of silk, feathers and lace.

Large amounts of perfume continued to hide the poor washing habits of people at this time. A new scented toilet water called Eau de Cologne was introduced from Germany and became very popular – as it still is today.

Men wore accessories, too, especially the silk cravat, which was tied loosely around the neck. Members of the aristocracy always carried a sword – one reason why arguments quickly turned into dangerous duels.

It was fashionable for men's hair to be long and curly. Many people wore wigs.

GETTING DRESSED

Getting dressed in the 1700s must have been a nightmare. A wealthy women would certainly have needed the help of a couple of servants.

Women's underwear was as important to their appearance as proper foundations are to a house! The wide skirts of fashionable gowns were supported by a panier, an enormous framework of metal hoops that must have been very uncomfortable to wear. In fact, a new style of chair was introduced at this time – rather like a bench; it was the only thing women could sit on! No doubt in the privacy of their own homes women wore smaller paniers or relaxed in a comfortable negligé.

On top of the panier was the gown's delicate underskirt, decorated perhaps with a deep frill. It contrasted beautifully with the silk or velvet gown that was worn open at the front and richly decorated with bows, borders and artificial flowers.

Cushions were tied onto the panier to form armrests!

Women's waists were laced tightly to contrast with the fullness of the skirt.

The shoes of this period were very delicate. They were made of silk and had high heels.

The extravagance of the gowns was matched by the enormous white wigs which were now in fashion. The wigs were so high that they brushed against the chandeliers – and sometimes even caught fire!

THE FRENCH REVOLUTION

The extravagant clothes worn by wealthy people were not copied by the French middle classes. They wore more practical clothes that were influenced by English fashion and the new ideas that were sweeping across France.

English fashion

The wealthiest people in English society were landowners who spent most of their time in the country. A country life requires practical clothes – the sort that can be worn on horseback! For men, this meant comfortable overcoats, short waistcoats and simple trousers. For women, it meant looser gowns in which they could move more easily

The English style soon reached France. When Frenchman began wearing trousers they were laughed at by well-dressed aristocrats, who still wore short culottes. They called them 'sansculottes' – which means 'people without culottes'.

Revolutionary ideas

Exciting new ideas were spreading across France. The great writers and thinkers of the age were encouraging people to think for themselves and question things that till now they had blindly accepted. Ideas can be very powerful, and in France they helped to cause a Revolution in which the king lost his life, and the wealthy aristocracy their power.

It was only a matter of time before the French began to question the clothes they wore, and to think about their needs in a more practical way. Out went the panier, the heavy embroidery and the bright brocades. In their place came easier styles, practical colours and plainer, lighter fabrics.

Typical French dress

Hair styles
and hats
began to look
more natural.

A revolutionary *sansculotte*
wore a chemise and cravat,
a short waistcoat, a jacket
with pockets, long trousers
and clogs.

Low leather
shoes or soft
boots were
widely worn.

FASHION AND NAPOLEON

After the turmoil and horrors of the Revolution, life in France began to settle down. In 1799 the country was taken over by the great military leader Napoleon Bonaparte, who shortly crowned himself Emperor. One of Napoleon's ambitions was to revive the splendour of the court at Versailles, and with this in mind he instructed France's most famous tailor to design an 'Imperial' style of dress.

The fashion industry
Like Louis XIV before him, Napoleon had a good reason for wanting a fashionable court – he hoped it would boost the country's textile industry. He was careful to encourage fashions that used the most expensive fabrics – cashmere, satin, taffeta and velvet. In doing so, he helped the textile factories around his growing Empire to keep busy and productive.

Women's style
Women's gowns were simple and graceful. They had very low, round or square necklines, with high waists decorated with ribbons or embroidered belts – a style which is still known as 'the Empire line'.

Men dressed in the English style, and began to tie their cravat in many different styles.

The Empire style had little influence on the middle classes or on fashions abroad.

Poor people wore long trousers, a chemise and jacket, with wooden clogs stuffed with straw in the winter.

Sleeves were designed in a number of styles: some were short and were worn with long gloves to cover the bare arms; others were long and sometimes had gathers down to the wrist. Women's skirts fell into folds which were gathered at the back to form a train. Though graceful, these dresses must have been chilly to wear; no wonder women carried warm cashmere shawls wherever they went.

Men's style

Although well-to-do men began to wear knee-length culottes again, the middle classes preferred the simpler English style of dress. With a short jacket or long coat, they wore plain trousers that looked more like the styles we wear today. All in all, there was little decoration in men's dress – just the graceful knot of a silk cravat.

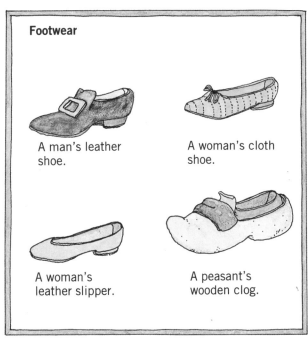

Footwear

A man's leather shoe.

A woman's cloth shoe.

A woman's leather slipper.

A peasant's wooden clog.

CLOTHES IN THE 1800s

Fashion seemed to stand still after the fall of Napoleon. There were very few new styles, and the clothes that people wore looked rather like those of the past.

Women's fashions

The graceful Empire line was soon given up in favour of dresses with a lower waistline. This revived the fashion for a slim waist, which in turn brought back the uncomfortable corset. Skirts began to widen again in order to contrast with the tight bodice of the gown, just as they had a century before. Sleeves, too, were worn much fuller, and were sometimes even padded.

Towards the middle of the century, high fashion was becoming popular again and people were looking for luxury. Women's skirts grew fuller and fuller until they were truly enormous. In the 1700s such skirts had been supported by a metal panier; in the 1800s they were supported by an underskirt made of crinoline — a stiff fabric of horsehair and flax. In fact, these full-skirted gowns came to be known as

Men's clothes remained fairly simple: long coats, or tailcoats, with a shirt and waistcoat over a pair of trousers. A walking cane was the height of fashion.

No woman left the house without a hat.

Shawls were still widely worn.

Dresses were brighter again, and decorated with bows and other trimmings.

Fashionable men wore a high-collared shirt and a colourful waistcoat with a long, dramatic cloak.

'crinolines'. They must have used many metres of cloth – especially when extra flounces became fashionable – and since wealthy women always prefer to wear expensive fabrics like silk, satin and taffeta, the cost of these dresses must have matched their size – enormous!

Fashion for all

More and more people were starting to wear fashionable clothes at this time. There were a number of reasons for this. Factories were beginning to make fabrics and accessories at a lower cost, which more ordinary people could now afford. Secondly, shops were springing up which sold fashionable ready-made clothes at reasonable prices. But most important of all, perhaps, was the invention of the sewing machine. With time, effort and some skill, most women could now afford to dress decoratively; fashion was no longer a privilege for the rich.

Small waists were fashionable. The corset must have been torture to wear.

A woman's skirt had as many as seven different layers, all made of different fabrics.

Uniforms of the day

politican — nurse — guard — fireman — postman — naval officer

jockey — railman — milliner — doctor — judge — miner

peasant — coachman — working woman — ballerina — cowboy — soldier

CENTURY OF THE ROMANTICS

A quieter style

While bonnets, bows and crinolines were hardly the simplest of clothes, the fashions worn by wealthy people in the 1800s were less extravagant than those worn a century earlier. It was still easy to recognise wealthy people, of course, by the quality and cut of their cloth, but they were less likely to look ridiculous or conspicuous. Even so, the upper classes enjoyed wearing something a little different and were always changing small details in their appearance and style. These changes were seized on by the popular fashion magazines of the day and brought to the attention of their readers.

The wealthy middle classes – people in business and industry – liked to copy the style of the upper classes, but not slavishly; they

wouldn't risk looking ridiculous. They wore the colours of the season, however; some of them had the most exotic names – like 'fainting rose' and 'dust of ancient ruins'!

The Romantic look

The 19th century (1800–1900) is often called the century of the Romantics. The word 'Romantic' is used to describe paintings, music, books and poems that express human feelings in an open and sometimes powerful way. These ideas were fashionable in the 1800s and began to change the way people dressed and behaved. For example, men were thought to have a romantic air if their hair looked wild and wavy; or they might take to wearing a French beret if they were the least bit artistic! Romantic ladies, on the other hand, were supposed to have pale skin and look rather weakly, so the women of the day always wore gloves and used parasols to avoid getting a suntan. They also wore veiled hats to create a sense of mystery. These fashions may seem ridiculous to us today – but think back over recent years. Doesn't fashion still try to change people – to make them seem something they're not?

Uniforms

In the past, people who worked in different professions had often worn particular colours and styles of clothes. It wasn't until the 1800s, however, that many different workers began to wear specially designed uniforms. The rail workers, who were employed on the new railway system, for example, wore a blue jacket and a flat peaked cap; bakers and milkmen wore white clothes and caps; and bricklayers and decorators wore pointed hats made of newspaper.

In well-to-do houses, domestic servants also began to wear uniforms. The cook wore a white jacket and cap; a maid wore a little white apron; and the butler wore a pinstripe suit. On special occasions, servants wore a splendid livery – a uniform that was designed for all the servants of a wealthy family, and which probably bore the family's coat of arms. Liveries were a status symbol – they showed the world how important you were. For many families, however, they became too expensive, and were replaced with plain, dark clothes, richly trimmed with golden cords and crested buttons.

Uniforms were worn by every class in society – even the criminal classes! Highwaymen who stopped carriages and robbed passengers of their jewels and money wore a black cloak, gold chains and a pointed hat trimmed with ribbons. And a common thief could always be identified by a rather smart pair of yellow gloves!

Children's clothes were becoming less formal. Boys wore short jackets and long trousers, and were often dressed in sailor suits. Girls wore shorter dresses than their mothers.

Evening gowns
were soft and
flowing, and had
low necklines.

Women's daytime clothes were getting simpler.

The elegant
gentleman wore a
Chesterfield
overcoat, with a
top hat and cane.

A CHANGING WORLD

Changes in society

Society had always been made up of different classes of people, depending on their wealth and power. In the past the aristocracy had been the most important class in society. Since the 18th century, however, these noble families had felt their power slipping away from them. They were still wealthy, of course, and were much admired, but their influence was growing weaker. It was the wealthy middle classes who now called the tune. They had built up huge fortunes; their industries employed thousands of people; and they helped to keep their country wealthy and productive. No wonder they were now the most important people in society.

Below them was the huge mix of ordinary people who worked in a wide range of jobs and professions, hoping one day to have the comfortable life of the middle classes.

Society was changing in another way, too. Women were becoming restless in the sheltered world of the home. They wanted a life in the outside world – a more active life, like men's.

Women never went out without a bonnet. There was a wide range to choose from at the milliners.

A fashion for all classes

In this mixed society there were many different people with many different needs. The fashion industry tried to suit them all, and there was now a larger range of clothes on offer than ever before.

For women, the crinoline was out of fashion and had been replaced by a much narrower skirt with a bustle – a pad which made the skirt puff out from behind. The bodice was still narrow, however, and women still suffered the tight squeeze of a corset.

City shops were bursting with ready-made clothes. For the daytime, women's styles and fabrics were becoming simpler and more practical: a jacket rather like a man's, a high-collared shirt, and a long skirt with a belt. For evening wear, dresses were still very feminine, with low necklines and flowing trains.

Men's jackets were becoming shorter. Men now wore overcoats outdoors, particularly a new style called the Chesterfield which had concealed buttoning. In the evening, elegant men wore black dinner jackets with a white shirt, along with a top hat and cane.

Men's clothes were becoming simpler and plainer. They dressed in black, grey, brown or blue.

THE END OF THE TAILOR

By the early 1900s the shops that sold ready-made clothes were doing a roaring trade. New shops called department stores were now opening in the larger towns and cities. They sold everything from clothes and hats to toys and plates. For the first time in their lives, customers could go in, look around, try this and that and leave without buying anything. It must have seemed a delicious freedom.

Mass-produced clothing

Great changes were taking place in the way clothes were made. Now that the sewing machine had been invented, clothes factories could produce large quantities of identical garments in different sizes and colours. This was the beginning of mass-produced clothes.

Many people still used the services of tailors and seamstresses, of course. The wealthiest people looked to their tailors to create highly fashionable styles; and many middle-class people still preferred having their clothes made especially for them – 'made to measure' as it is called. Most tailors realised, however, that for most ordinary people their services would soon be a thing of the past.

For gentlemen, English tailors were considered to be the finest in Europe. The best shops were all in one London street – Savile Row.

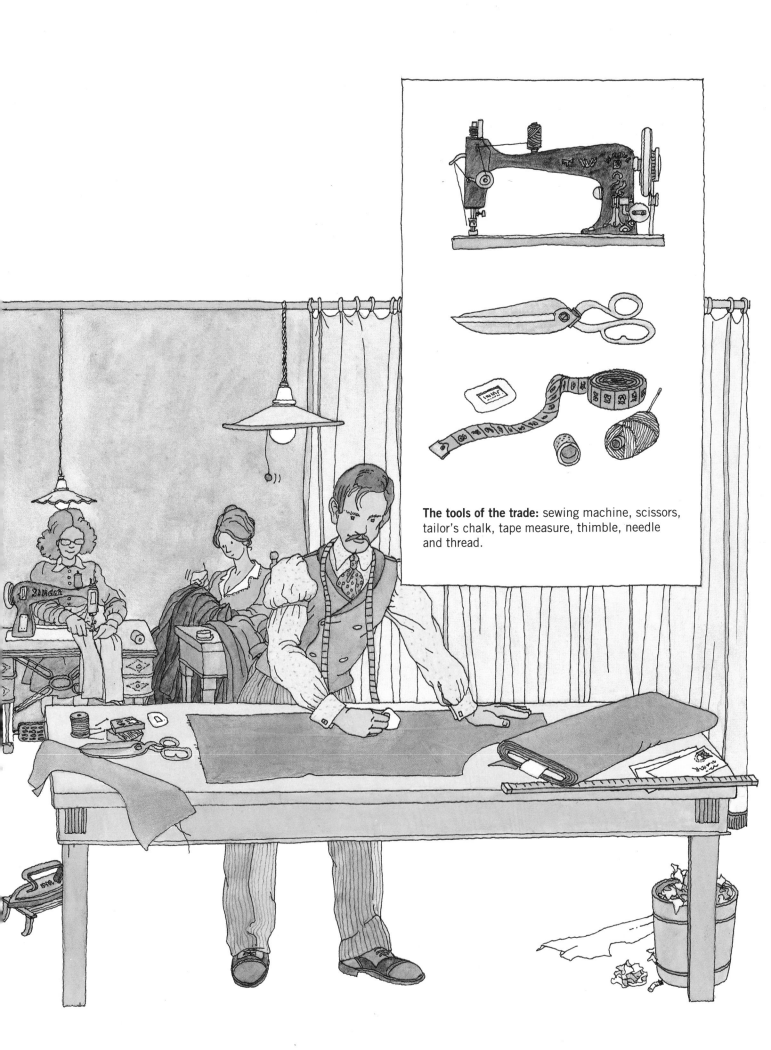

The tools of the trade: sewing machine, scissors, tailor's chalk, tape measure, thimble, needle and thread.

Fashionable style before the First World War.

THE MODERN WOMAN

It was women's clothes, not men's, that now began to change. At the beginning of the 20th century (1900–2000) wealthy women were still squeezing into tight corsets and wearing very dressy gowns with fringes, frills and cascades of lace. Their accessories were just as extravagant: ropes of pearls, long fur wraps and the most enormous hats.

Women in the War

The start of the First World War in 1914 brought many changes to the lives of women. As thousands of men left the country to fight, women took over their jobs in the factories. For many, it was their first real taste of independence.

Once the war was over, women continued to live a more active life. They needed simpler, more practical clothes – shorter skirts, freer styles, and shoes with sensible heels. Their hairstyles and hats became simpler, too. They even started to cut their hair!

The early 1900s were the last days of the corset.

After the First World War, women wore shorter skirts
and more comfortable styles.

Women began to wear trousers, and to dress like men
– a style they had seen in American films at the cinema.

GLOSSARY

accessory The extra items that complete a person's appearance. Hats, shoes, bags and fans are all accessories.

alum A natural substance that is found in the ground. It was used in ancient times for tanning animal skins.

Arab The word used to describe the Arabic-speaking people of North Africa and Arabia (in the Middle East).

archaeologist A person who studies the buried remains of ancient times.

aristocracy The noble families who make up the highest class of society.

aristocrat A member of the aristocracy.

barbarians The name given to the different tribes which invaded the Roman Empire in AD 300–400.

beret A round woollen cap which is considered typical of artists and Frenchmen.

bodice The top half of a woman's dress, usually close-fitting.

bolero A woman's short jacket which is left open at the front.

braid A decorative edging which is sewn on to material.

breeches Short trousers for men. They were very popular in Europe during the Middle Ages.

brocade A heavy silk material with a raised pattern.

bustle A pad or framework which was worn under a woman's skirt to make it puff out behind. Bustles were worn in the 19th century (1800–1900).

butler The most important male servant in a house.

carding To comb, clean and prepare wool, ready for spinning.

cashmere A fine soft wool which is made from the hair of a type of goat in Kashmir, India. Cashmere is very light and very warm.

chandelier A highly ornamental holder for candles or lights which hangs from the ceiling of a room.

chemise A linen undershirt.

Chesterfield A style of gentleman's overcoat.

civet A strong-smelling liquid which is obtained from the civet cat, and used in making perfume.

civilisation A human society which has a written language, and a high level of art, religion, science and government.

coat of arms A group of pictures which is painted on a shield, and used by a noble family as their special sign.

conspicuous Very noticeable.

cork The light springy bark of the cork oak tree, often used to seal wine bottles.

corset A very tight-fitting piece of underwear, worn by women to make them look slimmer.

cotton The thread or cloth which is made from the soft white hairs of the cotton plant.

cravat A soft necktie for men.

crinoline A stiff underskirt worn by women in the 19th century (1800–1900) to keep skirts stiff. It was first made of crinoline material – a mixture of horsehair and flax. It was later made of metal wires.

culottes Tight knee-length breeches for men.

damask A decorative fabric of silk or linen. The pattern is woven into the cloth itself, and can only be seen in a good light.

Dark Ages The period in the history of Europe from about AD 500–900.

distaff A long stick which was once used as a tool for spinning wool.

doublet A man's tight-fitting waistcoat. It was usually padded.

duel A fight with guns or swords, arranged between two people because of an argument.

embroidery Decorative sewing on a fabric.

farthingale A petticoat with whalebone hoops which was worn by women to make their skirt stand out at the hips.

feudal system A system where people are given land and protection by a lord, in return for their work and help in time of war. The feudal system was widespread in Europe during the Middle Ages.

fibres The threads that make up the stalks of many plants and the coats of animals.

flax A plant whose fibres are used to make linen.

fleece A sheep's woolly coat.

flimsy A very light and thin material.

flint A very hard stone that was used by the earliest people to make tools.

formal A stiff and correct way of behaving.

furrier A person who makes fur garments.

gem A precious stone.

haberdasher A shopkeeper who sells pins, thread and other items for dressmaking.

hide The skin of an animal which is used to make leather.

hose Tight-fitting leggings which were worn in the Middle Ages.

linen A type of cloth which is made from flax.

livery A special uniform for all the servants who work for the same person.

loincloth A loose covering for the lower part of the body, usually worn by men in hot countries.

loom A frame on which thread is woven into cloth.

manufacture To make something in large quantities with the help of machines.

mass-produce To make something in large numbers to the same pattern or design.

medieval Belonging to the Middle Ages.

muff A short tube made of cloth or fur which protects your hands from the cold.

musk A strong-smelling substance which is obtained from the musk deer, and used in making perfume.

Muslim A person who believes in the religion of Islam, which was started by Mohammed.

muslin A very fine thin cotton material.

negligé A light, comfortable robe which was worn by women in the home in the 1700s.

nomads People who do not live in one fixed place but travel about, often to find grass for their animals.

ornate Very highly decorated.

panier A framework of metal hoops which women wore under their petticoat to keep their skirts wide and rigid.

parasol A sunshade.

pharaoh The ruler of Ancient Egypt.

pinstripe A dark cloth with a regular pattern of thin white lines.

pleat A narrow fold in a piece of cloth which is then flattened.

practical Suitable and convenient to use.

preserve To prevent something decaying. Tanning the skin of an animal is a way of preserving it.

printing press A machine that prints books, newspapers, and so on.

Renaissance The period in Europe between about 1300–1600, when artists returned to the classical ideas of Ancient Greece and Rome.

revolution A time of great, and sometimes violent, social change. The French Revolution in 1789–1790 removed the French king from the throne.

ruff A stiff white collar which was worn in Europe in the 16th century (1500–1600).

sash A length of cloth worn round the waist rather like a belt.

satin A smooth shiny cloth made mainly of silk.

serf A person who is so poor that he is forced to stay and work on his master's land.

severe Very plain and without any decoration.

shear To cut wool from a sheep's back.

silk A smooth soft cloth made from the long, silky threads of the silkworm.

smock A loose shirt-like garment to put over other clothes.

sole The flat, bottom part of a shoe.

sombre Dark and serious.

spindle A tool that was once used for spinning wool.

taffeta A thick, silky, rustling material often used to make women's petticoats.

tailor's chalk A white chalk used by tailors to make marks on a piece of material before cutting.

tan To preserve the skin of an animal and change it into leather.

textile industry All the work which is done by cloth-weaving factories.

toga A long loose garment worn by the citizens of Ancient Rome.

toilet water A light perfume.

train The part of a long dress that trails on the ground behind the wearer.

vassal A person who promised to serve and fight for a lord in the Middle Ages, and who was given land in return.

veil A covering of fine cloth for the head or face.

velvet A luxurious cloth which has a soft raised surface of cut threads on one side only.

vent A straight opening at the bottom of a coat, either at the sides or the back.

warp The threads which run along the length of a piece of cloth.

weft The threads which are woven across a piece of cloth.

whalebone A material taken from the jaw of whales which was used to keep things stiff and in a certain shape.

wimple A piece of cloth which was worn round the neck and face by women in the Middle Ages.

wrap A piece of material which is used as a covering, like a shawl.

INDEX

HOUSES

CLOTHES

COMMUNICATION

FOOD

TRANSPORT

TECHNOLOGY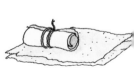